MYSTERIOUS WANDERERS

AN ANTHOLOGY OF INDIAN SNAKES

AVNIJA PANDEY

Contents

Contents

Foreword

Snakes are amongst the most fascinating, mysterious and unknown organisms on the planet.

But due to unawareness, people have a certain phobia against them, and they often end up unnecessarily hurting, or even killing these magnificent creatures. But why? All over the world, only 20% snakes are venomous, out of which only 7% are fatal to humans. Even many superstitions across the globe cause many species to come on the brink of extinction.

This may seem like a very small issue, but snakes too play a crucial role in the balance of nature. Cruelty to snakes is as serious as is cruelty to any other animal. Awareness amongst the population is absolutely necessary to end this. We all, every single one of us, must shoulder the responsibility to end false notions and superstitions, and to create awareness, that if we do not hurt them and leave them alone, they too will not hurt us. Their hurting us is all because of the damage we have inflicted upon nature and the Earth.

In this book, I have tried to do my bit to help save these beautiful critters by including essential information about snake species, the IUCN red list, types of scales present on a snake's body, threats to snakes and ways to distinguish between a venomous and non-venomous snake simply by looking.

Distiguishing Between A Venomous And Non-venomous Snakes Through Observation

i. There is an absence of pits in non-venomous snakes.

Pit represented inside circle, of a venomous snake.*PICTURE COURTESY: Britannica*

ii. Non-venomous snakes have rounded snouts, whereas venomous have slightly triangular ones.

iii. Non-venomous snakes have rounded pupils, whereas venomous have elliptical ones (called cat-eyed).

iv. The heads of non-venomous snakes are almost indistingushable from the remainder of the body, unlike venomous snakes, with clearly distinguishable heads.

v. There is an absence of fangs (hollow, venom-filled teeth) in non-venomous snakes.

vi. Non-venomous snakes are thin, and narrow as compared to venomous snakes, and are almost uniform in thickness. Venomous snakes are narrower at the ends.

vii. There is a double row of dorsal scales (refer chapter 23) near the tail in non-venomous snakes, whereas venomous snakes have a single row.

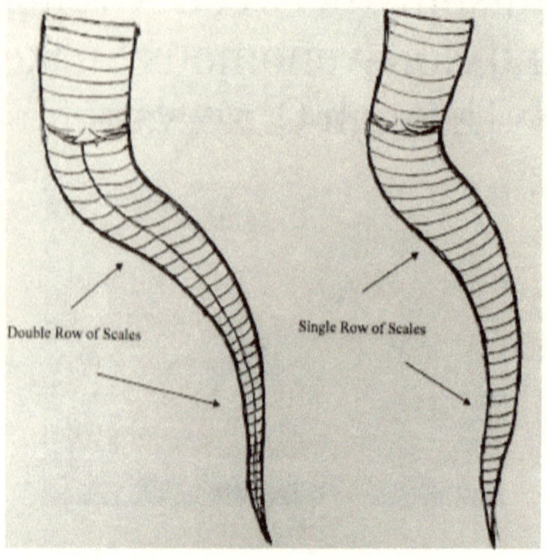

Venomous (left) and Non-venomous (right) comparision*PICTURE COURTESY: jbsrattles.com*

viii. In non-venomous snakes, the tail tapers into a point, whereas in venomous snakes it remains blunt.

CHAPTER I

AQUATIC RHABDOPS

Their back is olive greenish-brown with black spots. Their stomach is off-white in colour.

They are non-venomous snakes. They are found in the northern regions of the Western Ghats in Inida.

They are labelled as 'Not Evaluated' on the IUCN red list. Their scientific name is 'Rhabdops aquaticus'.

PICTURE COURTESY: Davidvraju (Wikipedia)

CHAPTER II

BOAS

I. Indian Sand Boa:

Their speckled body is brownish-red in colour. They have faint, black bands, more prominent towards the tail. Their head is wedge shaped, with a sharp slope like structure.

Their diet consists mainly of small mammals, especially rodents like rats, mice and squirrels. They may live up to 20 years. They are non-venomous snakes. They are endemic to India, Pakistan and Iran.

They are labelled as 'Near Threatened' on the IUCN red list due to superstitions and illegal wildlife trade. Their scientific name is 'Eryx johnii'.

HEADPICTURE COURTESY: AshLin (Wikipedia)

PICTURE COURTESY: Sagar khunte (Wikipedia)

II. Russell's Boa:

There is a dark brown, thick, wavy line running along their back, which tapers towards the head. The rest of their body is light brown in colour. Their head is brown-coloured.

They feed on small mammals and birds. They are non-venomous snakes, which kill through extreme constriction. They are native to South Asia.

They are labelled as 'Near Threatened' on the IUCN red list due to habitat loss and road kills. Their scientific name is 'Gongylophis conicus'.

PICTURE COURTESY: Sandilya Theuerkauf (Wikipedia)

CHAPTER III

BRAHMINY BLIND SNAKE

They are the smallest-known snakes in the world and resemble worms. Their stomach is paler in colour. Their body colour is variable, out of which, few are:

- deep gray
- whitish-gray
- yellow-ochre
- purplish-brown

They consume eggs, larvae and pupae of ants and termites. They are non-venomous snakes. They are native to Asia and Africa.

They are labelled as 'Not Evaluated' on the IUCN red list. Their scientific name is 'Indotyphlops braminus'.

PURPLISH-BROWN*PICTURE COURTESY: Davidvraju (Wikipedia)*

CHAPTER IV

CAT SNAKES

I. Beddome's Cat Snake:

They are slender snakes with a reddish-brown body and black patterns.

They consume dragon lizards, geckos, skinks and frogs. They are venomous snakes. They are endemic to the Western Ghats.

They are labelled as 'Least Concern' on the IUCN red list. Their scientific name is 'Boiga beddomei'.

PICTURE COURTESY: Jidnesh Doshi (Wikipedia)

II. Common Cat Snake:

Their body is yellow-ochre in colour. They have a white and black zigzag pattern on their back. The stomach is white in colour with spots along the sides.

They consume geckos, birds and frogs. They may live up to 15 years. They are mildly venomous snakes. They are native to South Asia.

They are labelled as 'Least Concern' on the IUCN red list. Their scientific name is 'Boiga trigonata'.

PICTURE COURTESY: Sagar khunte (Wikipedia)

III. Forsten's Cat Snake:

Their body is white with deep brown patterns. The top of their head is brown and lower part is white. There is a black streak behind the eyes. The stomach is white, spotted with brown.

They consume other snakes, lizards, rodents, birds and bats. They are venomous snakes. They are endemic to South Asia.

They are labelled as 'Least Concern' on the IUCN red list. Their scientific name is 'Boiga forsteni'.

PICTURE COURTESY: Davidvraju (Wikipedia)

IV. Tawny Cat Snake:

Their slender bodies are brownish-orange with the stomach slightly lighter.

They feed on birds, rodents, lizards and eggs. They are venomous snakes. They are endemic to South Asia.

They are labelled as 'Least Concern' on the IUCN red list. Their scientific name is 'Boiga ochracea'.

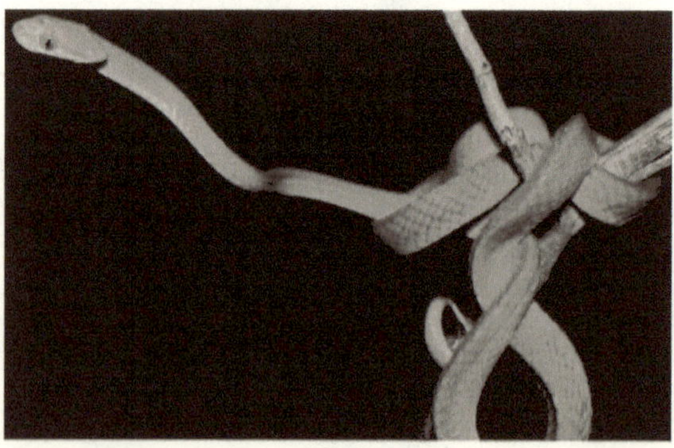

PICTURE COURTESY: Ashahar alias Krishna Khan
(Wikipedia)

CHAPTER V

COBRAS

I. Andaman Spitting Cobra:

Their back is greyish-black in colour with white between the gaps of the scales. Their stomach is light grey in colour with faint, black lines.

They feed on rodents, frogs and lizards. They may live upto 9 years. They are venomous snakes. They are endemic to the Andaman Islands of India.

They are labelled as 'Not Evaluated' on the IUCN red list. Their scientific name is 'Naja sagittifera'.

PICTURE COURTESY: Moinudheen (Wikipedia)

II. Indian Cobra:

Their medium sized back is brownish-ochre in colour. They have a large and impressive hood, behind which there is a black and white 'V' shaped pattern. Their stomach region is light ochre in colour with brown stripes.

They consume rodents, frogs and lizards. They may live up to 30 years. The males are heavier and longer than the females. They are highly venomous snakes. They are native to the Indian subcontinent. They are one of the 'Big Four' snakes of India.

They are labelled as 'Not Evaluated' on the IUCN red list. Their scientific name is 'Naja naja'.

HOOD*PICTURE COURTESY: Ganesh SahSudi (Wikipedia)*

PICTURE COURTESY: Saleem Hameed (Wikipedia)

III. King Cobra:

Their back is black with equally spaced white bands. Their stomach is brownish-orange. Also, there are triangular, black patterns and faded black stripes on the stomach. Their head is light brown in colour. Their hood is also black.

They feed on other snakes and lizards. They usually live up to 20 years. They are venomous snakes. They are endemic to South and Southeast Asia.

They are labelled as 'Vulnerable' on the IUCN red list due to habitat loss and poaching for meat, skin and Traditional Chinese Medicine. Their scientific name is 'Ophiophus hannah'.

PICTURE COURTESY: Michael Allen Smith (Wikipedia)

IV. Monocled Cobra:

Their speckled back is dark brown in colour, with a whitish, curved quadrilateral-shaped pattern with black spots inside. Their stomach is white with black stripes.

They feed on snakes, small mammals and fish. They may live up to 20 years. They are venomous snakes. They are found in South and Southeast Asia.

They are labelled as 'Least Concern' on the IUCN red list. Their scientific name is 'Naja kaouthia'.

HOOD*PICTURE OCURTESY: Biswarup Ganguly*
(Wikipedia)

AVNIJA PANDEY

*PICTURE COURTESY- yendoandando -
https://www.flickr.com/photos/yendoandando/
2875812514/ (Wikipedia)*

15

CHAPTER VI

CORAL SNAKES

I. Beddome's Coral Snake:

They are slender snakes. Their back is greyish-black and stomach is red. There are black spots towards the head.

They are venomous snakes. They are endemic to India.

They are labelled as 'Data Deficient' on the IUCN red list. Their scientific name is 'Calliophis beddomei'.

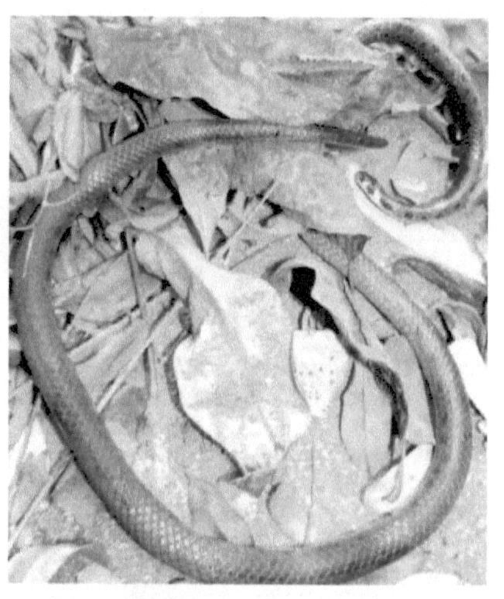

PICTURE COURTESY: Gachand (Wikipedia)

II. Bibron's Coral Snake:

They are either cherry-red or deep purplish-red in colour with black bands across the body. Their head is black above and body-coloured below.

They feed on other snakes. They are venomous snakes. They are native to India.

They are labelled as 'Least Concern' on the IUCN red list. Their scientific name is 'Calliophis bibroni'.

PICTURE COURTESY: Prasenjeet yadav (Wikipedia)

CHAPTER VII

DAUDIN'S BRONZEBACK

They are slender tree snakes. They have a bronze-coloured line running along their back. Their stomach region is yellowish in colour.

They feed on frogs, birds and lizards. They are non-venomous snakes. The males are shorter in length and brighter in colour than the females. They are found in South Asia.

They are labelled as 'Not Evaluated' on the IUCN red list. Their scientific name is 'Dendrelaphis tristis'.

PICTURE COURTESY: Saleem Hameed (Wikipedia)

SHOWING THE BRONZE-COLOURED LINE ALONG THE BACK*PICTURE COURTESY: Saleem Hameed (Wikipedia)*

CHAPTER VIII

EARTH SNAKES

I. Bombay Earth Snake:

Their body is purplish-black with yellow spots. The upper half of the head is purplish-black and the lower half is yellow. Their tail is speckled.

They are non-venomous snakes. They are endemic to Western India.

They are labelled as 'Least Concern' on the IUCN red list. Their scientific name is 'Uropeltis macrolepis'.

PICTURE COURTESY: Jidnesh Doshi (Wikipedia)

II. Elliot's Earth Snake:

They are very short snakes. Their body is reddish-brown in colour. There are dim yellow and blue stripes on the body. The regions near the tail and head are deep brown.

They consume Earth Worms and Caecilians. They are non-venomous snakes. They are endemic to India.

They are labelled as 'Least Concern' on the IUCN red list. Their scientific name is 'Uropeltis ellioti'.

PICTURE COURTESY: Davidvaju (Wikipedia)

III. Günther'sEarth Snake:

They are small, glossy snakes with reddish-brown hexagonal markings with whitish-grey in between the gaps of the markings. Their head is deep reddish-brown. There is a small, yellow streak on the neck. There are also a few yellow marks on the belly. They have a pencil-tip like tail.

They are non-venomous snakes. They are endemic to the Western Ghats of India.

They are labelled as 'Data Deficient' on the IUCN red list. Their scientific name is 'Plectrurus guentheri'.

PICTURE COURTESY: Davidvrju (Wikipedia)

CHAPTER IX

INDIAN RAT SNAKE

They have a thin body. Their back is greyish-black and their stomach is whitish in colour.

They consume rodents, other snakes, birds, eggs, lizards, amphibians and insects. They may live up to 11 years. They are non-venomous snakes. They are found in South and Southeast Asia.

They are labelled as 'Not Evaluated' on the IUCN red list. Their scientific name is 'Ptyas mucosa'

PICTURE COURTESY: Nireekshit (Wikipedia)

PICTURE COURTESY: Varkey Parakkal

CHAPTER X

INDIAN ROCK PYTHON

Their body is brownish-yellow in colour. They have crooked light brown patterns all over the body, which get smaller towards the tail. Their head is slightly reddish in colour.

They consume mammals, birds and reptiles. They are non-venomous snakes. The females are bulkier than the males. They are native to the Indian subcontinent and Southeast Asia.

They are labelled as 'Near Threatened' on the IUCN red list due to habitat loss and exploitation. Their scientific name is 'Python molurus'.

PICTURE COURTESY: Pratik Jain (Wikipedia)

CHAPTER XI

KEELBACKS

I. Buff Striped Keelback:

They are very distinctly coloured snakes. Their back is vertically striped with brownish and ochre colour. On top of the brownish stripes, there are black crossbars. The top of their head is grey and black. The region near the jaw is bright yellow. Their stomach is white with black spots.

They feed on amphibians, fish and geckos. They are non-venomous snakes. They are found in South and Southeast Asia.

They are labelled as 'Not Evaluated' on the IUCN red list. Their scientific name is 'Amphiesma stolatum'.

PICTURE COURTESY: AshLin (Wikipedia)

II. Checkered Keelback:

Their body is yellowish-brown. There are black crossbands which become fainter towards the tail. The region near the jaw is brighter.

They feed on small fish and water frogs. They are venomous snakes. They are endemic to India, Pakistan, Sri Lanka, China, Bangladesh, Afghanistan, Nepal, Myanmar, Australia, Taiwan, Indonesia, Malaysia, Cambodia, Vietnam, Thailand and Laos.

They are labelled as 'Not Evaluated' on the IUCN red list. Their scientific name is 'Fowlea piscator'.

PICTURE COURTESY: Dr. Raju Kasambe (Wikipedia)

III. Nilgiri Keelback:

Their back is brown with yellow spots. There are faint white streaks on the body. Their stomach is white with black line just under the eye.

They feed on toads. They are venomous snakes. They are found in the Western Ghats in India.

They are labelled as 'Least Concern' on the IUCN red list. Their scientific name is 'Hebius beddomei'.

PICTURE COURTESY: L. Shyamal (Wikipedia)

IV. Olive Keelback Wart Snake:

Their back is deep olive green and stomach is greenish-yellow in colour. There is a small reddish line on the stomach. They are often confused with the Olive Forest Snake (Rhabdops olivaceus).

They consume frogs, fish, crabs and tadpoles. They are non-venomous snakes. The reddish line described above is brighter in the males than in the females. The females are also longer than the males. They are found in India, Nepal, Sri Lanka and Bangladesh.

They are labelled as 'Least Concern' on the IUCN red list. Their scientific name is 'Atretium schistosum'.

PICTURE COURTESY: Gihan Jayaweera (Wikipedia)

V. Orange Collared Keelback:

Their body is whitish-grey with black zig-zag lines, between which there are white spots. There is an orange line on the neck.

They feed on frogs and toads. They are venomous snakes. They are found in India, Nepal, Bhutan, Bangladesh, Myanmar and China.

They are labelled as 'Not Evaluated' on the IUCN red list. Their scientific name is 'Rhabdophis himalayanus'.

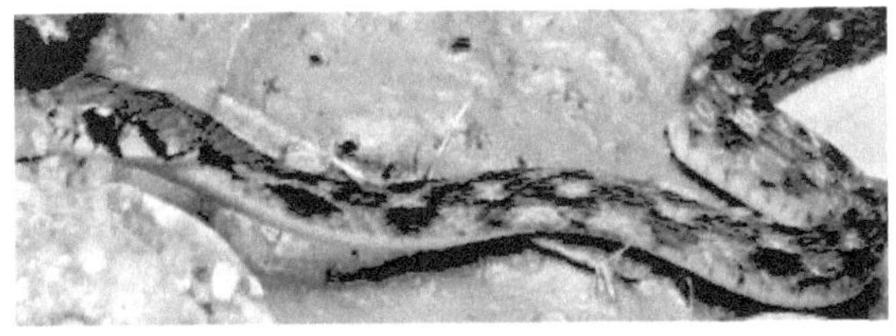

PICTURE COURTESY: The Reptile Database

CHAPTER XII

KRAITS

I. Banded Krait:

Their body has yellow and black bands. The top of their head is black, and the lower part is yellow in colour. They are the largest species of Krait.

They feed on other snakes, eggs, fish and frogs. They may live up to 13 years. They are venomous snakes. They are native to the Indian subcontinent, Southeast Asia and Southern China.

They are labelled as 'Least Concern' on the IUCN red list. Their scientific name is 'Bungarus fasciatus'.

PICTURE COURTESY: Davidvraju (Wikipedia)

II. Common Krait:

They have a blackish-brown body. Also, there are thin, white bands all over the body.

They feed on other snakes, rodents, lizards and frogs. They may live up to 17 years. The males are longer than the females. They are highly venomous snakes. They are native to the Indian subcontinent. They are one of the 'Big Four' snakes of India.

They are labelled as 'Not Evaluated' on the IUCN red list. Their scientific name is 'Bungarus caeruleus'

PICTURE COURTESY: Jayendra Chiplunkar (Wikipedia)

III. Greater Black Krait:

Their back is black in colour and stomach is whitish-yellow. They have a slightly triangular cross-section and a pointed tail.

They consume other snakes, small mammals, lizards, frogs and fish. They are venomous snakes and are endemic to South Asia.

They are labelled as 'Not Evaluated' on the IUCN red list. Their scientific name is 'Bungarus niger'.

PICTURE COURTESY: Jijomodak007 (Wikipedia)

IV. Lesser Black Krait:

They have a slender body. Their entire body is brown, varying from very light near the stomach, to dark on the back.

They are venomous snakes and are found in India, Bangladesh and Nepal.

They are labelled as 'Not Evaluated' on the IUCN red list. Their scientific name is 'Bungarus lividus'.

PICTURE COURTESY: Sp.herp (Wikipedia)

V. South Andaman Krait:

Their body is glossy, golden in colour. On their back and on the top of the head, there are large, black, oval spots. There are white patterns between the scales.

They consume water snakes and fish. They are venomous snakes and are found in the Andaman Islands of India.

They are labelled as 'Vulnerable' on the IUCN red list due to hunting, trading and habitat loss. Their scientific name is 'Bungarus andamanensis'.

PICTURE COURTESY: Coryphophylax

CHAPTER XIII

OLIVE FOREST SNAKE

Their slender bodies are olive greenish-brown in colour with small, black lines well-spaced everywhere across the body, except the head.

They feed on small, soft-bodied animals like rodents. They are non-venomous snakes and are endemic to the Western Ghats in India.

They are labelled as 'Least Concern' on the IUCN red list. Their scientific name is 'Rhabdops olivaceus'.

PICTURE COURTESY: avidvraju (Wikipedia)

CHAPTER XIV

PIT VIPERS

I. Bamboo Pit Viper:

Their stomach is bright green in colour. Their back region is bright green, but deeper than the stomach. They have a thin, white line on both sides of the body.

They feed on rodents, lizards, frogs and birds. They may live up to 6 years. They are venomous snakes with the females being larger in size than the males. They are endemic to Asia.

They are labelled as 'Least Concern' on the IUCN red list. Their scientific name is 'Trimeresurus stejnegeri'.

PICTURE COURTESY: Evan Pickett (Wikipedia)

II. Cantor's Pit Viper:

Their back is light brown, dark brown or green. Their stomach is cream or greenish in colour with brown spots under the tail.

They consume small mammals and birds. They are venomous snakes and are endemic to the Nicobar Islands of

India.

They are labelled as 'Not Evaluated' on the IUCN red list. Their scientific name is 'Trimeresurus cantori'.

PICTURE COURTESY: The Reptile Database

III. Himalayan Pit Viper:

They are the highest-living (living in the highest altitude) snakes in the world. Their back is brownish with lines. Their stomach is white with black and red dots.

They feed on small rodents, Centipedes and Millipedes. They are venomous snakes. They are found in the Himalayas (in India, Pakistan and Nepal).

They are labelled as 'Not Evaluated' on the IUCN red list. Their scientific name is 'Gloydius himalayanus'.

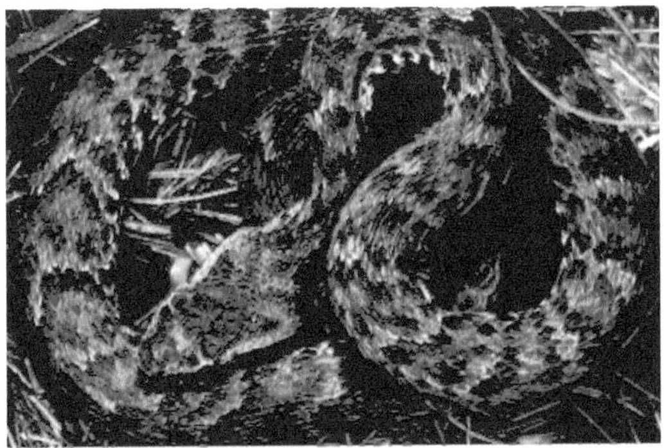

PICTURE COURTESY: The Reptile Database

IV. Horseshoe Pitviper:

Their body is dark brown with yellow-ochre 'U' shaped marks. The head is of a similar pattern as the body, except the lower jaw which has a greyish-white line.

They consume frogs, mice and lizards. They are venomous snakes and are endemic to the Western Ghats.

They are labelled as 'Least Concern' on the IUCN red list. Their scientific name is 'Trimeresurus strigatus'.

PICTURE COURTESY: Gachand (Wikipedia)

V. Indian Pit Viper:

Their back is deep green with streaks of black. Even the top part of the head, till the nose has a similar pattern. Their stomach region is yellowish-light green.

They feed on rodents, birds and lizards. They are venomous snakes and are native to South and North-East India.

They are labelled as 'Least Concern' on the IUCN red list. Their scientific name is 'Trimeresurus gramineus'.

HEADPICTURE COURTESY: Supratim Laha
(Wikipedia)

PICTURE COURTESY: Sagar khunte (Wikipedia)

VI. Jerdon's Pit Viper:

Their back is light green with black-bordered brown, irregular spots and black marks between the scales. Their stomach is white with black marks between the scales as well. The top of the head is fluorescent green with thick, black wavy lines.

They feed on rodents and frogs. They are venomous snakes and the females have more scales on the stomach than the males. They are native to India, Nepal, China, Myanmar and Vietnam.

They are labelled as 'Least Concern' on the IUCN red list. Their scientific name is 'Protobothrops jerdonii'.

PICTURE COURTESY: Stickpen (Wikipedia)

VII. Large Scaled Pitviper:

Their back is bright green in colour with a bit of black colour between scales. Their stomach is greenish-yellow.

They consume rodents, small birds, lizards and frogs. They are venomous snakes and are endemic to the Western Ghats in South India.

They are labelled as 'Near Threatened' on the IUCN red list due to habitat loss, hunting, trapping, roads and railways. Their scientific name is 'Trimeresurus macrolepis'.

PICTURE COURTESY: Seshadri. K. S (Wikipedia)

VIII. Malabar Pit Viper:

Many colour variations are known to exist, out of which some are as follows:

- rust-coloured with greenish
- emerald green, yellow and black
- blue, whitish, yellowish and black
- brown

They feed on mainly birds, shrews, frogs, lizards and mice. They are venomous snakes and the males have more scales on the stomach than the females. They are endemic to the Western Ghats of India.

They are labelled as 'Least Concern' on the IUCN red list. Their scientific name is 'Trimeresurus malabaricus'.

RUST-COLOURED WITH GREENISH*PICTURE*
COURTESY: Shyamal (Wikipedia)

EMERALD GREEN*PICTURE COURTESY: Umakant S*
Chavan (Wikipedia)

BLUE PICTURE COURTESY: Umakant S Chavan (Wikipedia)

BROWN PICTURE COURTESY: Nireekshit (Wikipedia)

IX. Merrem's Hump Nosed Pit Viper:

Their body is greyish in colour with black spots. Their stomach is yellowish or brownish and the end of their tail is reddish or yellow. Their snout is almost prism-shaped with the tip curved upwards.

They are venomous snakes and are endemic to India and Sri Lanka.

They are labelled as 'Not Evaluated' on the IUCN red list. Their scientific name is 'Hypnale hypnale'.

PICTURE COURTESY: Gihan Jayaweera (Wikipedia)

CLOSE-UP OF HEAD*PICTURE COURTESY: Vssekm (Wikipedia)*

X. Motuo Bamboo Pit Viper:

Their stomach is bright green, with lines seeming to divide the stomach in parts. Their back is bright green as well, but slightly deeper than the stomach. There are white and red lines on both sides of the body.

They consume small rodents, birds, frogs and lizards. They are venomous snakes and the males are longer than the females. They are endemic to India, Myanmar and China.

They are labelled as 'Data Deficient' on the IUCN red list. Their scientific name is 'Trimeresurus medoensis'.

PICTURE COURTESY: Rohit Naniwadekar (Wikipedia)

STOMACH*PICTURE COURTESY: Rohit Naniwadekar*
(Wikipedia)

XI. Northern White Lipped Pit Viper:

Their back is bright green, stomach is light green or yellow. The end of the tail is slightly brown.

They feed on small mammals, birds, frogs and lizards. They are venomous snakes. The males have a faint stripe on the sides, which the females lack. They are endemic to India, Bangladesh and Nepal.

They are labelled as 'Not Evaluated' on the IUCN red list. Their scientific name is 'Trimeresurus septentrionalis'.

PICTURE COURTESY: Trimeresurus87 (Wikipedia)

XII. Redtail Bamboo Pit Viper:

Their back is deep green with a bit of black colour between the scales. Their stomach region is bright green. The top of the head is deep green, and the lower part is bright green. A black line is present on both sides of the body.

They consume rodents, frogs, birds and lizards. They are venomous snakes. The black line is present in the males and may be present or absent in the females. They are found in South Asia and Myanmar.

They are labelled as 'Least Concern' on the IUCN red list. Their scientific name is 'Trimeresurus erythrurus'.

PICTURE COURTESY: Md Mehedi hasan456
(Wikipedia)

XIII. Salazar's Pit Viper:

Their back is deep green in colour, with red between the scales. There are red and white lines on both sides of the body. Their stomach is smooth, yellowish-green and their tail is red in colour.

They consume small mammals, birds, lizards and amphibians. They are venomous snakes. The females do not have stripes on the side of the body and a red tail, unlike the males.

They are labelled as 'Not Evaluated' on the IUCN red list. Their scientific name is 'Trimeresurus salazar'.

*PICTURE COURTESY: Aamod Zambre and Chintan Seth
(Wikipedia)*

CHAPTER XV

RACERS

I. Graceful Racer:

Their slender body is brownish-orange in colour. There are yellow-ochre crossbands, bordered by black on the portions of the body closer to the head. On the portions nearer to the tail, there are black stripes.

They consume small mammals, frogs and small reptiles. They may live up to 10 years. They are non-venomous snakes and are endemic to India.

They are labelled as 'Data Deficient' on the IUCN red list. Their scientific name is 'Platyceps gracilis'.

PICTURE COURTESY: Sagar khunte (Wikipedia)

II. Nagarjun Sagar Racer:

Their back is grey in colour with oval, brown spots bordered by black towards the centre of the body. Their tail is plain greyish, and head concentrated brown spots. Their stomach is white in colour.

They consume small mammals, birds and lizards. They are found in the Eastern Ghats and the Deccan Plateau.

They are labelled as 'Data Deficient' on the IUCN red list. Their scientific name is 'Platyceps bholanathi'.

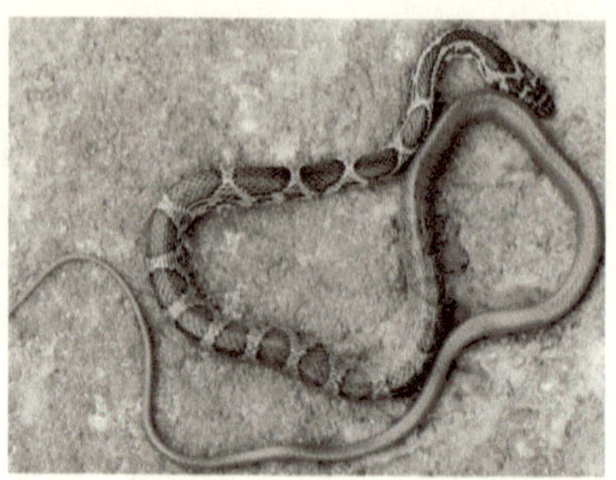

PICTURE COURTESY: The Reptile Database

CHAPTER XVI

RED CORAL KUKRI

They are slender, yellowish-orange snakes. The stomach region is slightly yellow in colour, with white colour near the throat. Their snout is bright, yellowish-orange.

They feed on insects and worms. They are non-venomous snakes and are found in India, Nepal and Bangladesh.

They are labelled as 'Least Concern' on the IUCN red list. Their scientific name is 'Oligodon kheriensis'.

PICTURE COURTESY: Sp.herp (Wikipedia)

CHAPTER XVII

SHIELDTAILS

I. Palni Shieldtail:

They are brownish-black in colour with golden stripes near the head.

They are non-venomous snakes and are endemic to the Western Ghats of India.

They are labelled as 'Least Concern' on the IUCN red list. Their scientific name is 'Uropeltis pulneyensis'.

PICTURE COURTESY: J. Jury (Wikipedia)

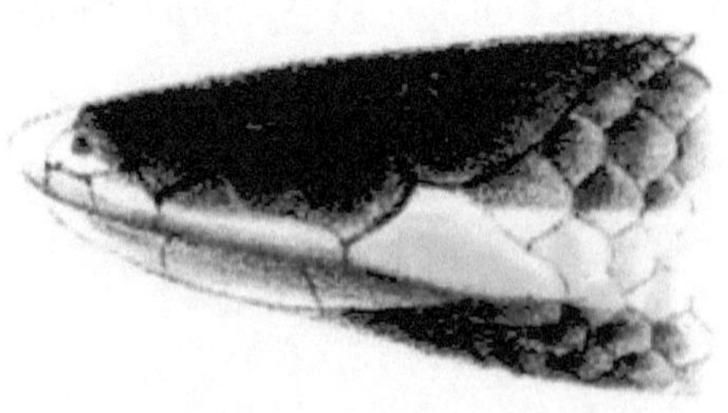

HEADPICTURE COURTESY: J. Jury (Wikipedia)

II. Phipson's Shieldtail:

They body is black in colour. There are yellow stripes on the sides of the body.

They consume Earth Worms and are endemic to India.

They are labelled as 'Vulnerable' on the IUCN red list due to habitat loss. Their scientific name is 'Uropeltis phipsonii'.

PICTURE COURTESY: Sinhu ramchandran (Wikipedia)

CHAPTER XVIII

VINE SNAKES

I. Asian Vine Snake:

The colour of the body is variable. Some of the colourations are:

- emerald green, whitish and bright green
- orangish-brown with diagonal yellow, white and black lines
- bright green
- whitish

They feed on small amphians and reptiles. They may live up to 12 years. They are mildly venomous. They are native to India, Myanmar, Bangladesh, Bhutan, China, Malaysia, Laos, Cambodia, Brunei, Philippenes, Indonesia, Thailand, Vietnam and Singapore.

They are labelled as 'Least Concern' on the IUCN red list. Their scientific name is 'Ahaetulla prasia'.

EMERALD GREEN*PICTURE COURTESY: Rushenb*
(Wikipedia)

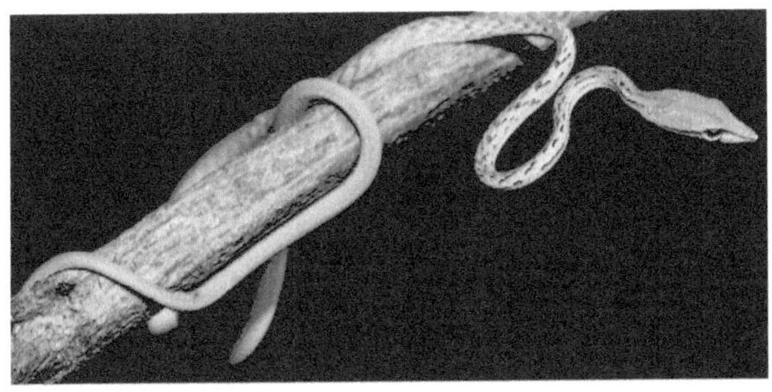

WHITISH*PICTURE COURTESY: Rushenb (Wikipedia)*

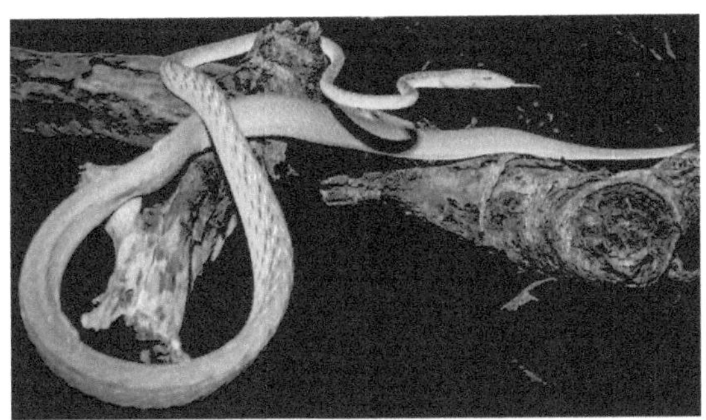

ORANGISH-BROWN*PICTURE COURTESY: Rushenb*
(Wikipedia)

BRIGHT GREEN*PICTURE COURTESY: Greg Hume*
(Wikipedia)

II. Günther's Vine Snake:

They are thin, slender snakes. Their back is deep green in colour. The back region (excluding the portion above the head) has black streaks between the scales. Their stomach is bright yellow-green. The region below the nostrils is white.

The above description pertains to the males, while the females are brown in colour. They feed on lizards and frogs, and are mildly venomous. They are endemic to the Western Ghats in India.

They are labelled as 'Near Threatened' on the IUCN red list due to habitat loss, hunting and trapping. Their scientific name is 'Ahaetulla dispar'.

PICTURE COURTESY: Davidvraju (Wikipedia)

CHAPTER XIX

VIPERS

I. Indian Saw Scaled Viper:

Their body is light yellow-ochre in colour. There are reddish-brown hexagonal patterns all over the body, covering it almost entirely.

They consume rodents, lizards, frogs, insects, scorpions, centipedes. They are venomous snakes and may live up to 20 years. They are native to the Indian subcontinent, the Middle East and Central Asia. They are one of the 'Big Four' snakes of India.

They are labelled as 'Not Evaluated' on the IUCN red list. Their scientific name is 'Echis carinatus'.

PICTURE COURTESY: Shantanu Kuveskar (Wikipedia)

II. Russell's Viper

They are yellow-ochre in colour with brown-black spots. Their body is thick, and tapers towards the tail.

They feed on rodents, reptiles, crabs and scorpions. They are venomous snakes and may live up to 15 years. They are native to India, Sri Lanka, Pakistan and Nepal. They are one of 'Big Four' snakes of India.

They are labelled as 'Not Evaluated' on the IUCN red list. Their scientific name is 'Daboia russelii'.

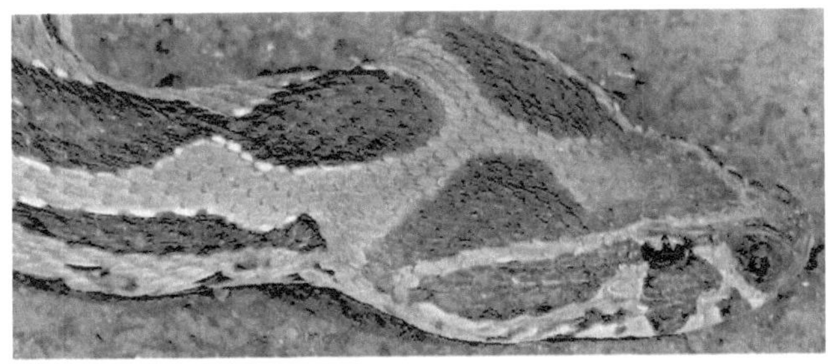

HEADPICTURE COURTESY: AChawla (Wikipedia)

PICTURE COURTESY: AChawla (Wikipedia)

CHAPTER XX

WATER SNAKES

I. Rainbow Water Snake:

Their body is golden in colour. The sides are bright, and the top and bottom are deeper.

They consume mainly fresh-water fish and amphibians. They are mildly venomous snake. They are endemic to India, Pakistan, Bangladesh, Nepal, Sri Lanka, Myanmar, China, Laos, Indonesia, Singapore, Malaysia, Cambodia, Thailand and Vietnam.

They are labelled as 'Least Concern' on the IUCN red list. Their scientific name is 'Enhydris enhydris'.

PICTURE COURTESY: Srikaanth Sekar (Wikipedia)

II. Siebold's Water Snake:

Their body is brownish-yellow in colour with black spots.

They feed on rodents and frogs. They are mildly venomous and are endemic to India, Bangladesh and Myanmar.

They are labelled as 'Least Concern. On the IUCN red list. Their scientific name is 'Ferania sieboldii'.

PICTURE COURTESY: Sp.herp (Wikipedia)

CHAPTER XXI

WOLF SNAKES

I. Indian Wolf Snake:

Their body is glossy, brown in colour. They have white 'X' shaped bands all over their body. Sometimes the colours are varied (uniform brown without band/ greyish-brown etc.). Due to their colouration, they are often confused with Common Kraits (Bungarus caeruleus).

They mainly feed on lizards, especially skinks, and frogs. They are non-venomous snakes, and the females are larger than the males. They are native to South and Southeast Asia.

They are labelled as 'Not Evaluated' on the IUCN red list. Their scientific name is 'Lycodon aulicus'.

PICTURE COURTESY: Davidvraju (Wikipedia)

II. Oriental Wolf Snake:

Their back is pale brown with yellowish-white crossbands across the body. Their stomach is brownish-white in colour and there is a yellow streak on the neck.

They feed on frogs and lizards, especially skinks and geckos. They are mildly venomous and are found majorly in South and Southeast Asia.

They are labelled as 'Least Concern' on the IUCN red list. Their scientific name is 'Lycodon capucinus'.

PICTURE COURTESY: Mark O' Shea (Wikipedia)

CHAPTER XXII

YELLOW–BELLIED SEA SNAKE

Their back is completely brown-black and stomach is yellow in colour. The sides have yellow and black curves and their tail is white and black.

They feed on majorly on fish and may live up to live 7 years. They are venomous snakes with the females being longer than the males. They are found in all tropical oceans except the Atlantic Ocean.

They are labelled as 'Least Concern' on the IUCN red list. Their scientific name is 'Hydrophis platurus'.

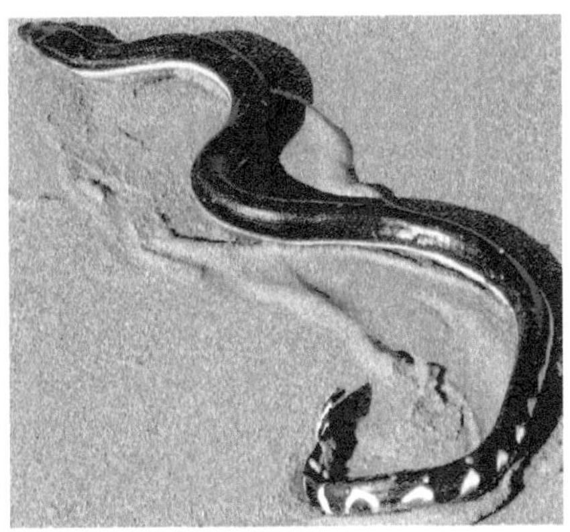

PICTURE COURTESY: Aloiza (Wikipedia)

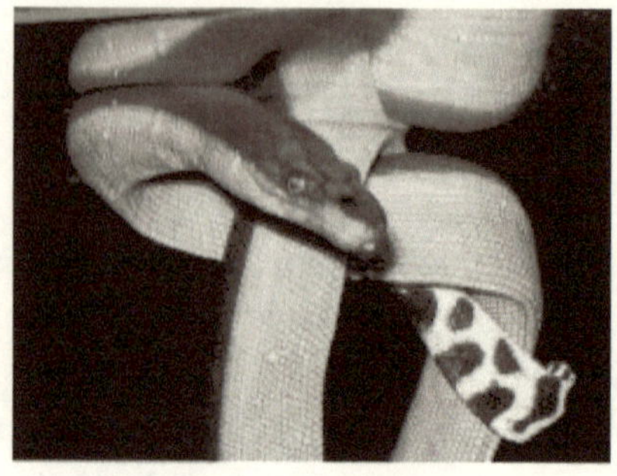

SHOWING DISTINCTLY-COLOURED TAIL*PICTURE*
COURTESY: Carpenter0 (Wikipdia)

CHAPTER XXIII

TYPES OF SCALES

Head Scales:

- Nasals - four scales (two on each side of the head) enclosing the nostrils
- Prenasal - outer nasal; nearer to the snout
- Postnasal - inner nasal; nearer to the eye
- Internasals - connect the nasals on both sides of the head
- Rostral - between the two prenasals on the tip of the snout
- Circumorbital - around the eyes
- Ocular - transparent scale covering eyes; also known as spectacle, brille or eyecap
- Preocular - circumorbital scales which are closer to the snout
- Postocular - circumorbital scales behind the eye
- Supraocular - circumrbital scales towards the top of the head
- Subocular - circumorbital scales just below the eye; may or may not be present
- Loreal - between the postnasal and preocular scales; absent in the 'Elapid' family of snakes
- Labials - along the lips
- Supralabials/ Upper Labials - labials on the upper lip
- Infralabials/ Lower Labials - labials on the lower lip
- Frontal - on top of the head; between the eyes; in contact with the supraocular scales
- Prefrontal - between the internasal and frontal scales

- Parietal - on the top of the head; just behind the frontal scale
- Temporal - below the parietal scale; behind the postocular scale
- Mental - ahead of the infralabials; near the lower jaw
- Anterior Chin Shields - two scales; between the infralaials of both sides
- Posterior Chin Shields - two scales; just below the anterior chin shields
- Gular - between the two posterior chin shields

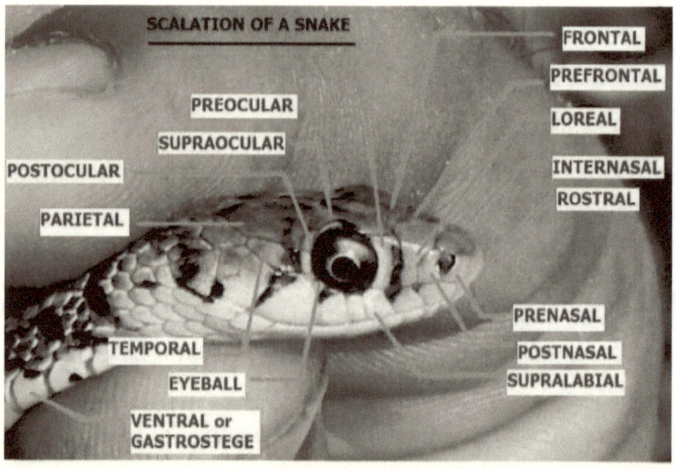

PICTURE COURTESY: AshLin (Wikipedia)

Body Scales:

- Ventral/ Gastrosteges - along the stomach, i.e. the underside
- Dorsal/ Costal - along the back, i.e. the upper-side

- Vertebral - uppermost row of scales on the back; along the vertebral column

CHAPTER XXIV

PERISHING OF SNAKES

There are many different threats to snakes all over the world. In order to understand the extent to which a snake is threatened, the International Union for Conservation of Nature (IUCN) shows the conservation status of each species.

There are 8 categories specified in the IUCN red list:a. Data Deficient (DD), meaning that there is not enough information about the particular species to tell their conservation status. They may or may not be endangered. Eg.- Beddome's Coral Snake Least Concern (LC), meaning that they are not in any sorts of danger. Eg.- Monocled Cobra Near Threatened (NT), meaning that they are in very little danger. Eg.- Indian Rock Python Vulnerable (VU), meaning that certain populations of the species are not safe. Eg.- Phipson's Shieldtail Endangered (EN), meaning that not many individuals are left. Eg.- March's Palm Pit Viper Critically Endangered (CR), meaning that we must start taking steps to ensure that the species is protected. Eg.- Santa Catalina Rattlesnake Extinct in the Wild (EW), meaning that they are no longer found in their natural hhabitat and are only found in captivity. Eg.- Kihansi Spray Toad Extinct (EX), meaning that it is too late to save them and not even a single individual is left. Eg.- Round Island Burrowing Boa

a. Data Deficient (DD), meaning that there is not enough information about the particular species to tell their conservation status. They may or may not be endangered. E.g.- Beddome's Coral Snake

b. Least Concern (LC), meaning that they are not in any sorts of danger. E.g.- Monocled Cobra

c. Near Threatened (NT), meaning that they are in very little danger. E.g.- Indian Rock Python

d. Vulnerable (VU), meaning that certain populations of the species are not safe. E.g.- Phipson's Shieldtail

e. Endangered (EN), meaning that not many individuals are left. E.g.- March's Palm Pit Viper

f. Critically Endangered (CR), meaning that we must start taking steps to ensure that the species is protected. E.g.- Santa Catalina Rattlesnake

g. Extinct in the Wild (EW), meaning that they are no longer found in their natural hhabitat and are only found in captivity. E.g.- Kihansi Spray Toad

h. Extinct (EX), meaning that it is too late to save them and not even a single individual is left. E.g.- Round Island Burrowing Boa

<u>Man-Made Threats</u>

I. Habitat Loss - Humans have been clearing out forests and other habitats of snakes to make space for homes, industries etc. But this leaves out very little area for wildlife to live in.

PICTURE COURTESY: tumblr 3.0 - Nitesh Gautam

II. Hunting and Poaching - Humans have been hunting snakes for medicine, meat, headgears etc. They have been killed as pests and sold as pets as well.

PICTURE COURTSY: Pinterest

III. Pollution - Humans have been polluting water bodies, grasslands and other habitats of snakes. The pollutants are either ingested by them or causes suffocation. Both ways, it kills them. Even oil spills in water are deadly for sea snakes.

PICTURE COURTESY: IQAir

IV. Climate Change - Global warming and climate change cause unusual temperature fluctuation, sea rise, floods, droughts, cyclones, more intense heat waves etc. It is happening at such a fast rate, that the wildlife is not able to adapt quickly enough. This is resulting in the decrease in their population, leading to endangerment and extinction of animals.

PICTURE COURTESY: New Scientitist

V. Unawareness- In many instances, people unknowingly hurt snakes. This is due to lack of awareness. Therefore, it is our responsibility to spread awareness

PICTURE COURTESY: Redbubble

<u>**Natural Threats**</u>

I. Natural hazards- Natural hazards can cause very high decline in their population.

PICTURE COURTESY: American Camp Association

II. Diseases- Just the way there are disease outbbreaks in humans, there are the same in snakes as well. These too can cause decline in their population. E.g.- Chronic Cryptosporidiosis occurred in a group of captive Australian snakes

**WE MUST NOT LET OUR LACK OF AWARENESS AND IGNORANCE LEAD US TO TAKE STEPS AGAINST THESE FASCINATING CREATURES.
IT WILL PROMPT GUILT AND REGRET WHEN IT IS TOO LATE**

CHAPTER XXV

SNAKE MAN OF INDIA

VAVA SURESH is known as the 'SNAKE MAN OF INDIA' for his life-threatening ways of rescuing and saving the life of more than 50,000 snakes which included many venomous snakes.

During his rescue missions, he has been bitten multiple times; with near-death experiences on a couple of occassions.

CHAPTER XXVI

THE BIG FOUR

Four species of venomous snakes have been identified as the cause of a majority of medically-significant snakebites, that is 90%, in the Indian subcontinent.

These four species are:

- the Indian Cobra (Naja naja) (Chapter 5)
- the Common Krait (Bungarus caeruleus) (Chapter 12)
- the Indian Saw-Scaled Viper (Echis carinatus) (Chapter 19)
- the Russell's Viper (Daboia russelii) (Chapter 19)

www.ingramcontent.com/pod-product-compliance
Lightning Source LLC
Chambersburg PA
CBHW021123130726
47988CB00003B/1139